Your Amazing Body

Skin

by Imogen Kingsley

Bullfrog Books

Ideas for Parents and Teachers

Bullfrog Books let children practice reading informational text at the earliest reading levels. Repetition, familiar words, and photo labels support early readers.

Before Reading

- Discuss the cover photo. What does it tell them?
- Look at the picture glossary together. Read and discuss the words.

Read the Book

- "Walk" through the book and look at the photos. Let the child ask questions. Point out the photo labels.
- Read the book to the child, or have him or her read independently.

After Reading

- Prompt the child to think more. Ask: What happens to your skin when you get hot? How about when you get cold? How do you think your skin helps you control your body temperature?

Bullfrog Books are published by Jump!
5357 Penn Avenue South
Minneapolis, MN 55419
www.jumplibrary.com

Copyright © 2018 Jump! International copyright reserved in all countries. No part of this book may be reproduced in any form without written permission from the publisher.

Library of Congress Cataloging-in-Publication Data

Names: Kingsley, Imogen, author.
Title: Skin / by Imogen Kingsley.
Description: Minneapolis, MN: Jump!, Inc., [2017]
Series: Your amazing body
"Bullfrog Books are published by Jump!"
Audience: Ages 5–8. | Audience: K to grade 3.
Includes index. | Identifiers: LCCN 2016059603 (print)
LCCN 2017000031 (ebook)
ISBN 9781620316894 (hardcover: alk. paper)
ISBN 9781620317426 (pbk.)
ISBN 9781624965661 (ebook)
Subjects: LCSH: Skin—Juvenile literature.
Human physiology—Juvenile literature.
Classification: LCC QM484 .K56 2017 (print)
LCC QM484 (ebook) | DDC 612.7/9—dc23
LC record available at https://lccn.loc.gov/2016059603

Editor: Jenny Fretland VanVoorst
Book Designer: Molly Ballanger
Photo Researcher: Molly Ballanger

Photo Credits: age fotostock: Swell Media, 7. Alamy: IAN HOOTON/SPL, 20–21. iStock: kali9, 18; Tanaphong, 19. Shutterstock: Levent Konuk, cover; JPC-PROD, 1; pakornkrit, 3; eveleen, 4; Asier Romero, 4, 5; smolaw, 5; Africa Studio, 6–7; Gelpi, 6–7; Melle V, 8–9; denniro, 10; 3445128471, 11; Kvitka Fabian, 14–15; John99, 16–17; Pakhnyushchy, 20–21; crystal light, 22; 3Dalia, 23tl; Sebastian Kaulitzki, 23bl; Warut Chinsai, 24. SuperStock: Blend Images, 12–13.

Printed in the United States of America at Corporate Graphics in North Mankato, Minnesota.

Table of Contents

Many Jobs	4
Parts of the Skin	22
Picture Glossary	23
Index	24
To Learn More	24

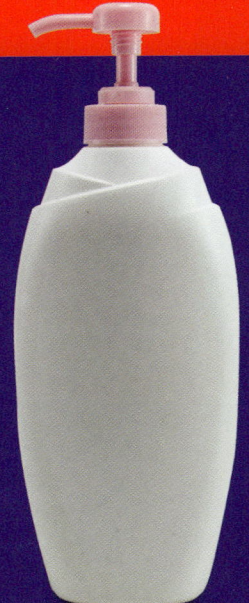

Many Jobs

What is the body's biggest organ?

Some people have dark skin.

Some people have light skin.

Others have a bit of both.

Skin has many jobs.

It holds body parts in.

It keeps dirt
and germs out.

It keeps your body at the right temperature.

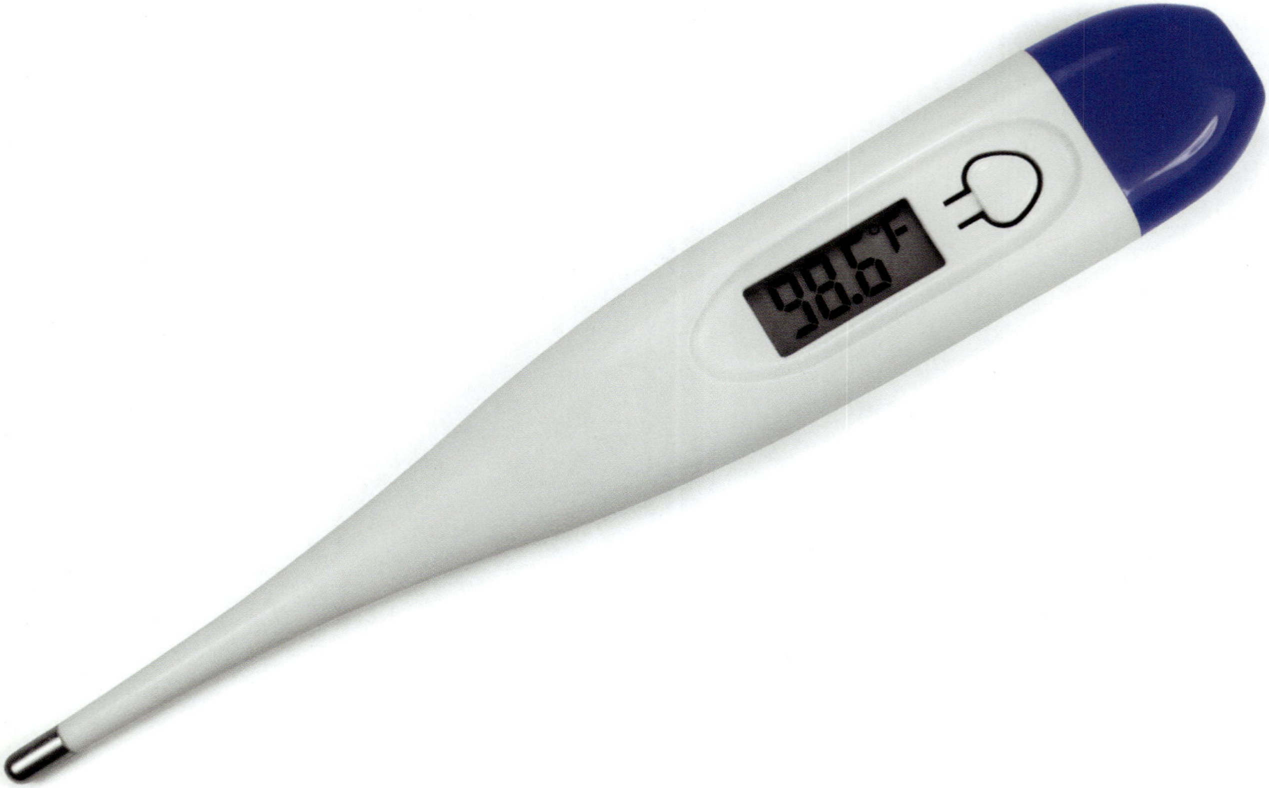

It is hot.
Dinesh sweats.
It cools him down.

Jo shivers. Brr!

She is cold.

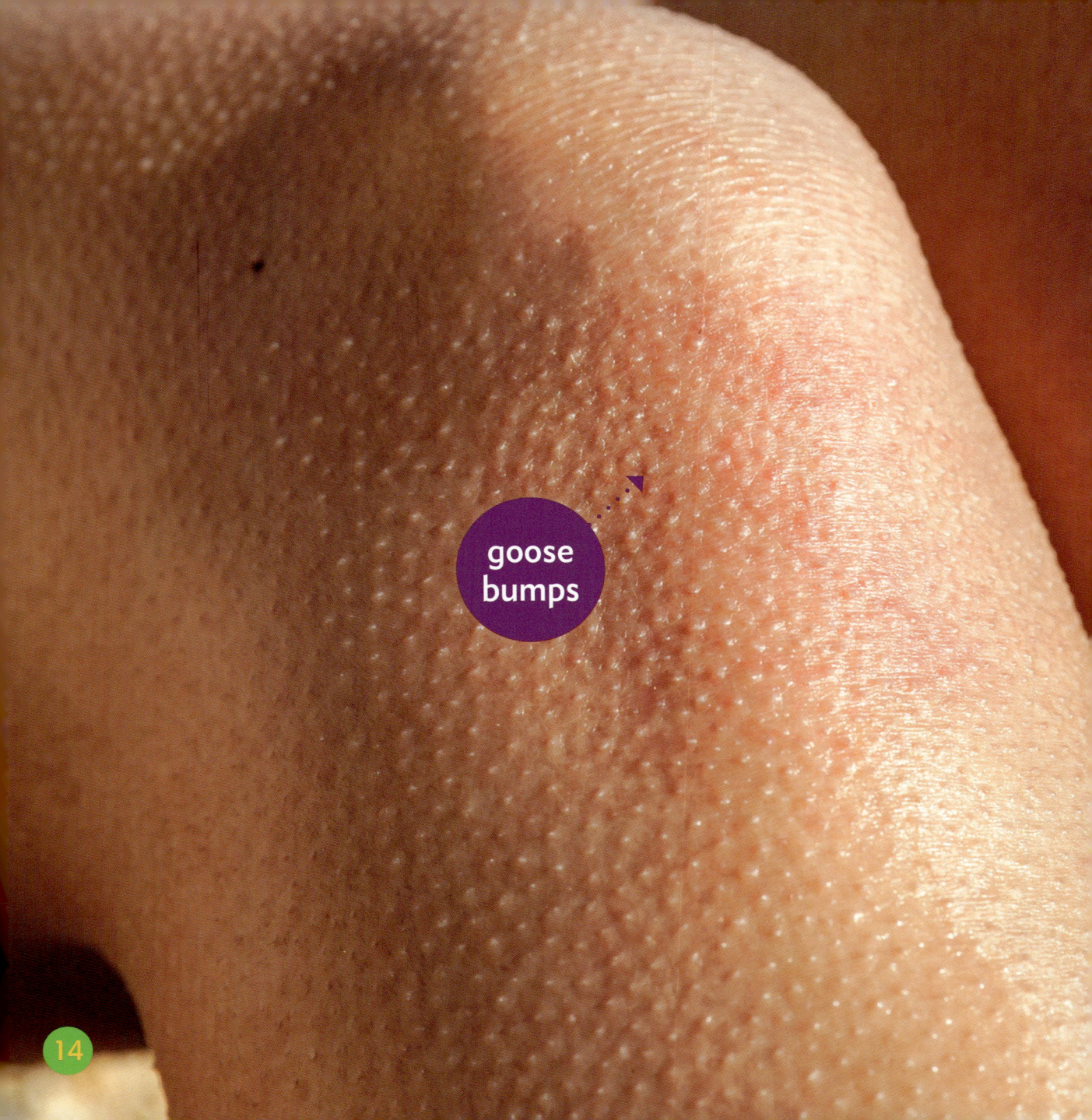

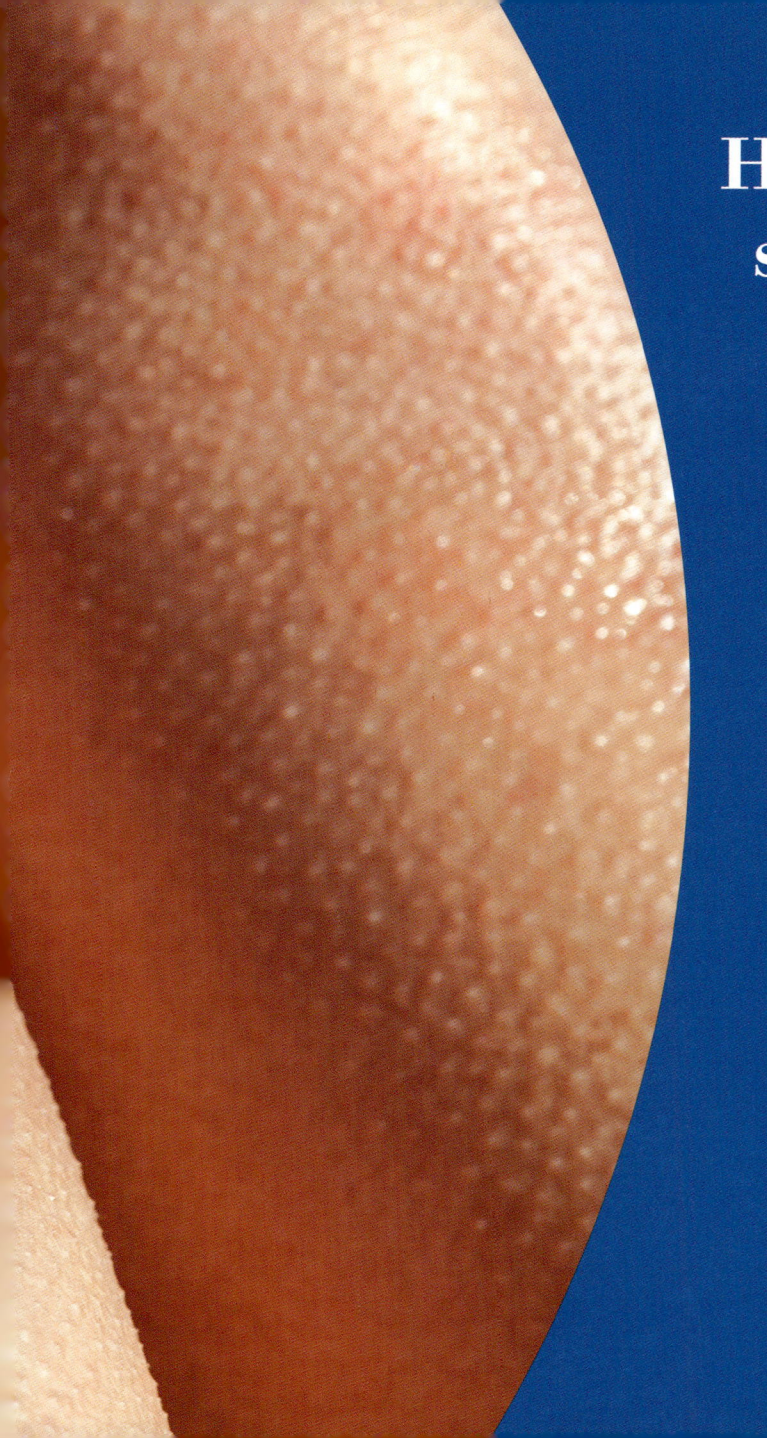

Hairs on her skin stand up.

Look!

They make goose bumps.

They keep her warm.

Skin gives you a sense of touch.

It works with your brain and nerves.

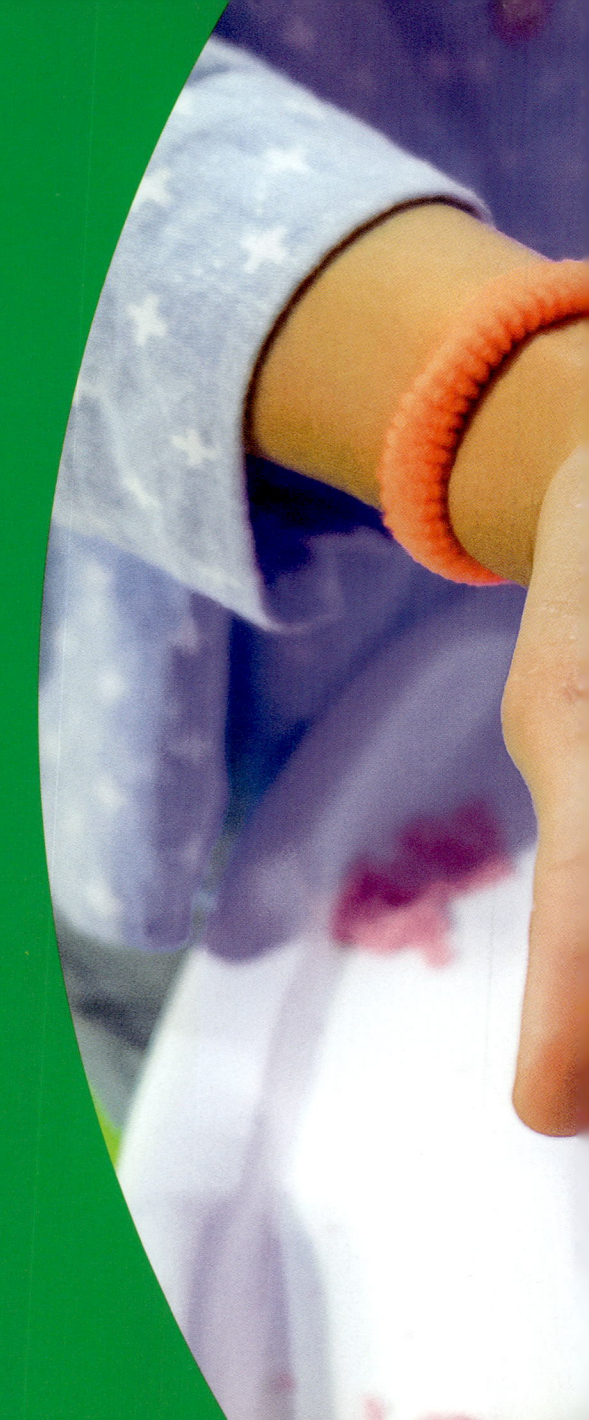

Is it hard or soft?

It is hot or cold? Your skin lets you know.

Skin is amazing!

Parts of the Skin

Skin has three layers. You see only the top layer. But lots goes on underneath the surface.

epidermis
The top layer where new skin cells are made.

dermis
The middle "stretchy" layer.

sweat gland
The place where sweat is made.

sebaceous gland
The place where skin oil is made.

subcutaneous layer
The third layer, made mostly of fat. It helps keep you warm and cushions you when you bump into things.

blood vessels
Tubes that carry food and oxygen to skin cells.

hair follicle
Where a hair grows.

22

Picture Glossary

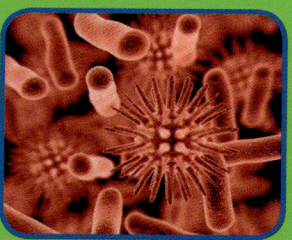

germs
Tiny living things that can make you sick.

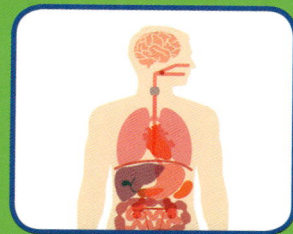

organ
A part of the body that has a specific function (the stomach, the brain, etc.).

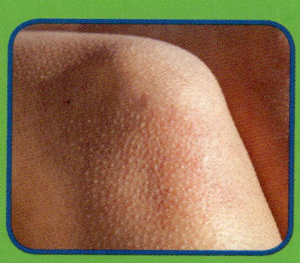

goose bumps
A roughening of the skin, usually caused by cold.

shivers
Shakes with cold.

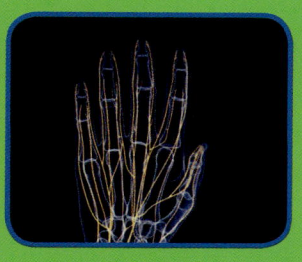

nerves
Parts of the body that send messages to the brain, allowing us to feel things.

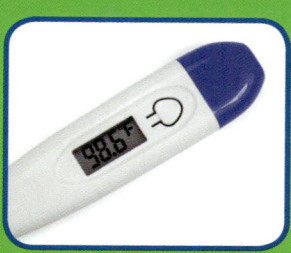

temperature
How warm or cold something is.

Index

brain 16
dark 7
germs 8
goose bumps 15
hairs 15
light 7

nerves 16
organ 4
shivers 12
sweats 11
temperature 10
touch 16

To Learn More

Learning more is as easy as 1, 2, 3.

1) Go to www.factsurfer.com

2) Enter "skin" into the search box.

3) Click the "Surf" button to see a list of websites.

With factsurfer.com, finding more information is just a click away.